A Word Is a Word... Or Is It?

Michael Graves

Scholastic

New York ● Toronto ● London ● Auckland ● Sydney ● Tokyo

Cover photo by Wayne Sproule

Design by Kathryn Cole

1st printing 1985   **Printed in Hong Kong**

Canadian Cataloguing in Publication Data

Graves, Michael F.
A word is a word — or is it?

(Bright ideas ; 2)
Bibliography
ISBN 0-590-71505-4

1. Children — Language.   2. Language acquisition.
3. Verbal ability in children.   I. Title.

LB1139.L3G72 1985   372.6   C84-099558-X

Contents

Words:
From one to a zillion in 18 years

Shortly before or after their first birthday, children are likely to utter their first word. The precise moment is often in doubt, of course. For one thing, children aren't always considerate enough to say their first word when an adult is present, especially one ready to note the details of the occasion. For another, first words usually appear after a period of extensive babbling of nonsense sounds, and true words aren't always easy to distinguish from babbling — a phenomenon not limited to children, cynics might observe. For still another, if recorded at all, first words are usually reported by proud parents, less than fully objective observers of their offsprings' accomplishments.

What do we know about first words? Linguists tell us they are likely to consist of a consonant sound followed by a vowel sound — something like *ma* — or of a repetition of the same consonant-vowel combination — like *mama*. Syntactically, the word is likely to represent a whole sentence. *Ball* may mean "Bring me a ball," "That's a ball," "Throw the ball" — though not likely "I'm having a ball." And semantically, the first word will probably represent a broader meaning than does the similar adult word. *Juice* may be used to refer to milk, water, and anything else children drink. Nor is the first set of meanings children assign to a word all that predictable. One boy often cited as an example used *wawa* to refer first to dogs, then to all animals and soft slippers, and finally to the picture of an old man dressed in fur.

As exciting as it is, the first word is not likely to open a floodgate of verbiage. During the

Water, water everywhere — and different ways to describe it.

Illustrative essay by Werner Zimmerman.

1

following three-month period, children may learn no more than an additional fifty words. At this time, their speech is likely to consist exclusively of single words, each representing a sentence or even a string of sentences. Most parents know this and often reply to a word with an elaborate response that contains the assumed meaning of the word. One traveling salesman I know would come into the house on Friday night after a week's absence and respond to his enthusiastic toddler's "Daddy" with something like "Yes, Daddy's home again. I'm tired but I'm happy to see you too. How is my little one? Did you look after your mother?" The child would usually respond to all this with a satisfied "Daddy," as if the adult's talk were a big accomplishment.

But after about three months, the floodgates open indeed. By the time children enter first grade, their phonological systems are largely complete: they can recognize and produce virtually all the sounds of the language into which they were born. They even know much of its grammar. Average six-year-olds can understand and produce a large percentage of the almost infinite number of sentence patterns in their language.

But they haven't progressed as far in the accumulation of vocabulary. How many words do they know? Estimates for children entering school range from 2000 to over 20,000, but there is no way (yet) to put confidence in a specific figure. The important point is that even if the larger figure is accepted there are a lot more words to be learned.

Someone has estimated that the total number of words used in school materials up to grade twelve is around 100,000. No one needs to learn every word that appears in print, of course; many of them are extremely rare. But everyone needs to learn a goodly number. The question is, which ones? And how does one learn them?

The importance of vocabulary

Before I address these key questions, I need to consider one other: why I think words are so important. I've spent about fifteen professional years on the learning and teaching of vocabulary. Why?

The simple answer is, I find words fascinating. They constitute a complete history of the ideas that people throughout the ages have considered important enough to name. They are also very tangible elements for instruction; I can tell when I've taught a word, and I can tell when students have learned. Few instructional goals offer such simplicity or certainty.

My private reasons may or may not sound convincing. So I'll invoke a public body of educators, the authors of a report on the teaching of vocabulary commissioned by the National Council of Teachers of English (NCTE). On page 7 of *The State of Knowledge about the Teaching of Vocabulary*, this august body has said:

> The importance of vocabulary is daily demonstrated in schools and out. In the classroom, the achieving students possess the most adequate vocabularies. Because of the verbal nature of most classroom activities, knowledge of words and ability to use language are essential to success in these activities. After schooling has ended, adequacy of vocabulary is almost equally essential for achievement in vocations and society. These are not simply the opinions of the writers of this report; they are truisms noted by even the casual investigator. Certainly, doing as much as possible toward the development of vocabularies having depth and breadth becomes a natural function of the school and teachers.

Since the authors specifically state that these observations are not simply opinions, we must assess the weight of their evidence. There is a good deal, some of which I will summarize briefly:

- A strong relationship between vocabulary knowledge and intellectual ability has been noted for over a hundred years. Psychologists have suggested, in fact, that a vocabulary test could serve as a short version of an intelligence test.

- Word knowledge is strongly related to reading comprehension. Studies that have attempted to identify the components of reading comprehension have repeatedly found word knowledge to be the major component.

- Formulas that assess the difficulty of texts virtually always include a word factor, and the word factor is invariably the most powerful predictor in the formulas.

- Simplifying the vocabulary of texts has been shown to increase readers' comprehension, in some cases markedly.

- Preteaching difficult vocabulary of texts has been shown to increase comprehension and recall of those texts.

- Long-term vocabulary instruction has been effective in improving students' ability to comprehend what they read.

- It has been demonstrated repeatedly that judgment about the quality of a piece of writing is influenced strongly by the vocabulary in it.

- The direct teaching of a set of words useful in writing about a specific topic has been shown to constitute particularly strong preparation for writing. Writing by children who have been prepared this way has been judged to be markedly superior to that of children who did not receive such instruction.

An impressive list of evidence indeed. No wonder an author once observed that if we were to learn one word a day over a period of a year, and then consciously use those words in speech and writing, we would be perceived to be better educated, more important, more powerful, taller, and morally superior. *Being* all that is better, of course, than merely being perceived to be, but I at least am intrigued by the possibility of bettering my image, and I've started on my own daily word program.

I should also say that my editor told me to keep this book simple. No academic jargon, no five-syllable words, no obscure references. He insisted that its purpose is not to have readers know how smart the writer is, but rather to help teachers help students.

I once heard of a book salesman for whom English was a second language. He would wake up in the morning and immediately consult his dictionary for an obscure word, then use it at appropriate times during the day, in the hope of being challenged. If he was, he would quickly arrange a little bet — say a delicate lunch with some white wine. I wouldn't be surprised to learn that man is now both rich and obese.

The words the crafty fellow used undoubtedly came from the *Oxford English Dictionary,* an English language institution, a monument to the importance of words. Scotsman James Murray worked on its first edition for decades, and if you want to become possessed of a story about a man possessed with words, read his biography *Caught in the Web of Words.*

Some preliminaries to teaching vocabulary

If you are convinced, as I am, that vocabulary is important, it makes sense to ask what is being done and what can be done to promote vocabulary growth.

Any answer to that question must include a consideration of grade levels. In the primary grades, a good proportion of the day is devoted to learning how to read. The selections used in most primary-grade reading series are written specifically for those series. The vocabulary in them is carefully controlled, and in most reading programs a substantial amount of time is spent on directly and systematically teaching students to recognize the deliberately chosen set of words introduced in the readers. During the first three years, then, vocabulary instruction occupies a central position in the curriculum.

After the primary grades, however, most reading series begin using selections that weren't specifically written for them and that don't contain controlled vocabularies. They stop systematically introducing a specific set of words and instead simply teach some of the new words that come up in the reading selections. Also, as some researchers have pointed out, the methods of teaching vocabulary at the higher grade levels tend to be quite weak.

Moreover, vocabulary programs separate from reading programs are extremely rare. Schools do, of course, continue to devote a great deal of time to spelling, in both elementary and secondary grades, but learning to spell words is not the same as learning new words. While I certainly don't agree with Mark Twain, who claimed to have nothing but disdain for those who could spell a word only one way, it seems to me that vocabulary instruction ought to be given equal time with spelling.

So here I enter my first plea: beginning in the primary grades and continuing all through school, vocabulary instruction that is well motivated and that has a definite direction and focus ought to be a vital part of the curriculum in every school.

I have a system I use. It doesn't guarantee success, because only teachers teach, not systems. But "vocabulary" is a word that covers a variety of related things, and variety is best managed by a system. Variety? Yes, since there are different types of words students need to learn and different tasks they face in learning them. Over a number of years, several colleagues and I have worked out a system for classifying the relationship between words and learners. It is useful in selecting which words to teach and in deciding just what is meant by "teaching" a word.

In the next chapter, I'll give an overview of this system. Then, in the following four chapters, I'll describe each of the four types of vocabulary identified in the system. Finally, in the last chapter, I'll spell out classroom implications for teaching different types of words.

Vocabulary:
A word is a word — or is it?

Much of the difficulty in learning a word depends on the relationship between that word and the reader. The system I'm suggesting was designed to classify the possible relationships. Kenneth Goodman originally suggested part of it, and Judith Boettcher, Rebecca Palmer, Randall Ryder and I modified and elaborated on it during some bitterly cold Minnesota winters. In its present form, the system identifies four types of vocabulary:

Sight Words
Words which are in students' oral vocabularies, but which they can't read.

New Words
Words which are in neither the oral nor the reading vocabularies of students, but for which a concept is available (in known words) or for which one can be built fairly easily.

New Concepts
Words which are not in students' oral or reading vocabularies, for which they don't have a concept, and for which a concept is not easily built.

New Meanings
Words which are already in the students' reading vocabularies with one or more meanings, but for which additional meanings need to be learned.

The reason for not including examples at this stage is that the same word may well be in four different categories for four different people — a point that will be illustrated in a moment. I will provide examples later, in the chapters that deal with each type of word in detail.

First, some general characteristics of the system should be noted:

8

1. On the whole, Sight Words are easier to teach than New Words and New Concepts, and New Words are easier to teach than New Concepts. The last category — New Meanings — can be easy or difficult in varying degrees, depending on factors I'll mention later.

2. The system is relative rather than absolute. It classifies words and concepts according to the individual's prior knowledge of those words and concepts. Take *bog,* for example. For a student from Louisiana, the word is probably a Sight Word, since he or she has often heard mother say: "Don't play in the bog in your clean clothes."

For a Florida child, *bog* might be a New Word. Say he or she lives near a swamp. All you will have to explain is that a bog is like the wet, spongy ground in and around a swamp. Such an explanation doesn't provide a fully developed concept, of course, but if a story states that Lewis and Clarke were delayed for three days because they had to cross a large bog, the child will be able to read on with sufficient retention of meaning.

But for someone from Arizona, *bog* is likely to be a New Concept. Arizona is short on bogs and swamps, and the idea of wet, spongy ground is totally foreign to the children's experience and hard for them to imagine. It will take more than a brief explanation to get the concept across.

3. The third characteristic is a limitation of the second. The fact that the same word bears different relationships to different people does not mean that each classroom becomes a Tower of Babel. Within more or less homogeneous classrooms, with students of roughly the same age and from roughly the same background, the relationships between specific words and prior knowledge will be similar for all. The children in such classrooms will face similar learning tasks. The less homogeneous a classroom is, the more varied vocabulary learning tasks will be. This is important to remember, especially for the multi-ethnic classrooms likely to be found in large cities like Los Angeles, Toronto, and Sydney.

hy'drō·pow'er

Sight Words:
Getting your sights trained on words

Preschool learning

Most parents don't directly teach preschoolers to read many words, but those they do teach will likely be Sight Words — words that are already in their children's oral vocabularies but that they don't recognize in print. *MacDonalds, Stop, Police,* and *Bus* will be picked up quickly from the environment. One family I know played an alphabet sequence game while driving. The children would spot each letter of the alphabet in turn, from *A* to *Z,* and more than letters were learned in the process. Usually, and as it should be, this preschool instruction is low-key, consisting largely of parents' answers to children's questions about specific words, or of a few words put up on the refrigerator with magnetic letters.

Such words as *cat, moon,* and *bird* will come easily as children follow along while their parents repeatedly read favorite books aloud to them. Between being read to and picking up environmental language, some young children learn a fair number of Sight Words. However, most enter school with a very limited reading vocabulary.

Primary-grade learning

For most children, learning to read Sight Words is the major vocabulary learning task in the early school years. I noted earlier that estimates of their oral vocabularies range up to 20,000 words. I have reasons to believe it's closer to 2000, but even that lower estimate is an impressive number. However, most first-graders can read only a few of those words.

Primary-grade texts introduce words slowly. To simplify the learning task, they almost exclusively use words already in students' oral vocabularies. For teachers, then, the major task in teaching reading vocabulary is teaching Sight Words. Over the first three years of school, students are likely to encounter 2000 to 3000 Sight Words in their readers, and some additional ones in their other texts. Examples of Sight Words in primers are *fast, home,* and *two.* Typical for grade-one readers are *got, many,* and *surprise.* Second-grade students may encounter *job, quite,* and *stretch.* Third-grade readers may include *amaze, machine,* and *weigh.*

Sight Words can be classified in many different ways. One useful distinction is between those that are decodable using phonics skills and those that are not. Of course, as students develop more mature phonics skills, words will shift from one category to another. For instance, if a student has not mastered the "silent -*e*" rule, the word *lake* will not be readily decodable. But once that rule and the letter-sound correspondences involved have been learned, *lake* is a phonics cinch. Things get tougher for a word like *bought,* especially when compared with one like *bough.* Indeed, a significant number of words will never be fully decodable using phonics, because they contain irregular and seldom occurring letter-sound correspondences. *Language* and *laughter* are good examples.

Average and above-average readers in the intermediate grades

The pattern for early grades is clear. For beginning readers, teachers (and helpful parents) must teach the majority of Sight Words encountered. But as students' phonics and other word identification skills increase, fewer and fewer Sight Words need to be taught. By the time average students get to fourth grade or so, they have become sufficiently skilled at using structural analysis, context clues and phonics, singly or in concert, to identify most of the Sight Words they encounter.

There will always be difficult Sight Words, of course. *Hors d'oeuvre* might well be familiar to students from middle-class families. Some would even be able to name several, readily point out the ones they'll devour and the ones they despise, and respond quite matter-of-factly to a question like "What are you having for hors d'oeuvres tonight?" However, even these sophisticates might have trouble recognizing the word in print, and phonics won't cut the mustard. So, if that word were included in a selection, you might simply write it on the chalkboard and then pronounce it. Parents should not be surprised if at times their largely independently reading offspring ask about words of this sort when they encounter them in print.

Nevertheless, for average and above-average students beyond the primary grades, Sight Word problems are infrequent. A recent study indicated that average fourth-graders could read 96% of the words they could understand when they heard them read. Even adults will now and then encounter words they know perfectly well but don't recognize in print and will have to pause before thinking "Ah, so that's what that looks like" or "So that's how that's spelled." One word that hit me that way recently was *cacophony* — although I have to admit that it's not exactly a word I "know perfectly well."

Below-average readers at all grade levels

Poor readers face a different situation beyond grade four. They recognize only a limited number of words on sight, since they have very poor word recognition skills. They are often forced to ponder over words as they read, and they spend a good deal of time and energy identifying them — which severely interferes with comprehension.

Comprehension can occur only when the vast majority of words the reader encounters are recognized without conscious attention, instantaneously and automatically. So here is a second important plea: poor readers should be taught a set of basic words they are likely to encounter in their reading, and they need to reach a level of automaticity in recognizing those words.

Where should those words come from? Most appropriately, from the basal reading series the students are using, beginning with the words found most frequently. Start with the word lists from the earliest readers and test students' ability to pronounce the words included. Teach them those they can't pronounce.

"Testing," I want to emphasize, can consist merely of asking students to pronounce the words, for they already know their meanings. You could start with a subset of 20 words randomly selected from among those used at a particular level. If students recognize those, chances are good they will know the rest of the list also. If, on the other hand, they can identify only 15 of them, then they probably need to be tested on all the words to determine which ones need to be taught.

"Teaching" simply means showing the words in question and pronouncing them. The simplicity of this task makes it possible to involve parents. Chalkboards, pieces of paper, word games, and word lists are the most common tools.

After the words at the lower levels have been mastered, you can proceed to higher and higher levels. Exactly how many words should be screened and taught, if necessary, is hard to say. It seems reasonable to deal eventually with the basic vocabulary of a series through grade three. Judging by most popular series, that would include about 2500 words.

For students whose reading does not include or go much beyond a specific reading series, other sources of vocabulary must be found. A number of word lists are available. The shortest, easiest, and probably best known is the Dolch List of 220 Basic Sight Words, first composed in 1945. This is a list of extremely frequent words, especially function words such as *of, the, how,* etc. Most students will have mastered them by the end of grade two. However, since they make up about 60% of the words in typical texts, it is crucial that older students who don't know them learn them.

A considerably longer list is the Spache Revised Word List (1974), containing about 1100 words — including, as you might expect, nearly all of the 220 Dolch words. This is an updated version of a list developed in the 1930's, and is used in conjunction with the Spache Readability formula, the most commonly used formula for primary-grade materials. The more words from a selection not found on the word list, the higher the readability level, so it's not surprising that most of the primary-grade material and much of the material written for older students who do not read well employ words almost exclusively from the list. If, then, teachers can guarantee that students know the words on this list, they can identify a number of books in which the vocabulary, at least, will not constitute a stumbling block.

Time for a third plea: why not get your school or district to identify a list of about 1000 words and make every effort to ensure that *all* students can respond automatically to them by a certain grade level. The 1000 words would be those appearing most frequently in students' reading material, and the vast majority would be Sight Words. "Ensuring" would include screening all students and teaching the words to those who don't know them.

It should be possible for an elementary school staff to ensure that virtually all students have mastered such a word list by the end of grade six, and for junior high teachers, by the end of grade seven, to catch and handle the few who would have slipped through the elementary screens. The confidence that all students had mastered a specific basic vocabulary would be extremely useful to teachers in selecting materials for lower-performing students. And since teaching Sight Words is such a simple and straightforward task, parents can definitely assist with it.

Is it worth considering teaching an even larger body of Sight Words? My instincts tell me so, but I could be wrong. Remember that the purpose would simply be to ensure that readers would be able to recognize, without thought or effort, the vast majority of words they encounter in their reading materials. That's not all there is to reading, of course, but without it, comprehension is seriously impaired. If you are convinced of the worth of larger word lists, let me point you to two possible sources.

The Harris-Jacobson list contains about 6000 words that appear in basal readers and other reading materials for grades one to six. They are listed by the grade level at which they are first widely used. It would be relatively simple to select a school-district list of 3000 words or so, probably the 3000 words that are introduced earliest.

The American Heritage Word Frequency Book is based on a frequency count of words used in third- through ninth-grade materials, and lists words by frequency. For example, the most frequent word is *the*, the tenth most frequent is *it*, the hundredth is *know*, and the thousandth is *pass*. You could select a subset of this list, again perhaps 3000 or so.

The process of identifying words to teach from longer lists would be the same as that for the shorter lists, and as with the shorter lists, relatively few students would need to be taught many words. Lists of 3000 words or so would probably be most useful at the junior high level, where teachers might attempt to make sure that all students have mastered them by the end of grade nine. Again, parents' assistance would be extremely helpful.

In conclusion, I want to reiterate two points. First, while I do recommend ensuring recognition of a basic set of words, I emphasize that relatively few students will need to be taught Sight Words beyond the primary grades. Most students learn to read the majority of words in their oral vocabularies during their first years in school. Second, Sight Words do need to be taught so that students' responses to them are automatic. Too frequent use of word analysis will thwart reading fluency and retard comprehension.

New Words:
Creating them was Adam's task

Learning New Words — ones that are not in their oral or reading vocabularies, but for which they have available concepts — is the greatest word-learning task students face once they leave the primary grades. No one really knows how many words the average grade twelve student knows, probably between 20,000 and 60,000. But this we do know: the vast majority of words students must learn will be New Words.

How many? Which? How?

Those of you who are strong on rolling up sleeves and getting organized, no matter how forbidding the task, will immediately start calculating requirements. Let's see, with 3000 words by the end of grade three, that leaves somewhere between 17,000 and 57,000 for the next nine years. That's a minimum of 1888 per year. With roughly 180 school days, that means at least 10 each day, and maybe more than 30. Impossible!

Precisely! Don't even think about it.

That doesn't mean that none should be taught. Rather, the size of the task implies that teachers, and parents whenever possible, need to employ some judicious combination of two elements. First, they need to ensure that students themselves have strategies that will enable them to deal independently with at least some of the New Words they encounter. Second, they need to identify and teach those New Words that students have problems dealing with independently, or which are particularly important for some reason.

Teaching students general strategies for dealing with unknown words — how to use such things as phonics, structural analysis, context, and the dictionary — will not be discussed here, although mastery of three of them is exceedingly important for learning New Words. However, your knowledge of the competency of your students in these skills will have a bearing on which New Words you decide to teach.

General strategies

The first point I want to make about general strategies for dealing with unknown words is that many students will already have mastered them in the primary grades. The second is that for New Words phonics, usually the most highly stressed strategy, is useless. (That strategy is useful, it should be noted, in teaching Sight Words, but with New Words we are specifically concerned with meaning.)

Simply decoding an unknown word — sounding it out — gets students nowhere, since by definition New Words are not part of their aural or oral vocabularies. In an article in the *Minnesota English Journal*, Rebecca Palmer has aptly described the lack of help students get from sounding out such a word. She uses the word *lackadaisical* as an example:

> Say, for instance, the students come across the word *lackadaisical*, one which they have neither spoken or written before. Though they may be able to sound out the word and break it into its various parts correctly, coming up with something like "lak-a-day-zi-kal," this alone is not enough to provide the meaning. From sounding out *lackadaisical*, students are likely to come up with meanings for words that sound like parts of it. Does *lackadaisical* have to do with a missing daisy? Or a missing day? Is it anything like dazed or a day's cycle? No. The problem with understanding *lackadaisical* doesn't lie with discovering its sound; the problem is to discover its meaning.

That leaves the other three general strategies:

using structural analysis, context clues, and the dictionary. If students have not mastered them, they need to be taught. Moreover, *real* mastery is necessary, to enable them to tackle New Words on their own.

Which New Words should be specifically taught? There are three steps for deciding. First, you need to get some idea what words students are likely to learn by themselves. Second, you need a set of criteria for selecting which words to teach. Third, you need to identify specific words.

How to identify New Words to teach

Are teachers good at identifying words students know or don't know? My own research and my work with teachers has told me that some are excellent at it, some terrible, and most somewhere in between. Luckily, there are some very good tools to help us all.

Edgar Dale and Joseph O'Rourke have written a text called *The Living Word Vocabulary,* the culmination of over forty years of vocabulary studies by Professor Dale. This very useful tool came out of vocabulary tests administered to students in grades 4, 6, 8, 10, 12, 13, and 16, tests that included about 43,000 items testing some 30,000 words. Each item was administered to students at various grade levels in an attempt to discover at what level between 67% and 84% of the students correctly identified the meaning of the word.

The book presents the word tested, the meaning tested, the grade level at which 67-84% of the students knew the particular word-meaning combination, and the exact percentage of students at that grade level who correctly answered the item. For example, *gratify* was tested for one meaning, and *pose* for four. Here are the results:

Word	Meaning	Grade	Score
gratify	to please	8	67%
pose	to sit for an artist	4	80%
pose	to pretend	6	80%
pose	a position	8	84%
pose	to present	12	78%

As can be seen, the test indicates that 67% of the eighth-grade students tested knew the word *gratify* with the meaning "to please." Each of the entries for *pose* provides similar information.

With one exception, *The Living Word Vocabulary* provides precisely the information we need for our purposes. That is, it answers the question "What percentage of my students are likely to know this word with this meaning?" Moreover, research has shown that the predictions are quite accurate.

I suppose we can never have all we want, but it would have been nice had the book contained one more piece of information. It tells us that 67% of eighth-graders will know *gratify* is "to please," but it doesn't specify how many older or younger students are likely to know it. The best we have is the authors' assertion that word-meaning combinations are likely to be known by about 10% fewer children at each successive lower level and 10% more at each successive higher level.

How about a little test to see how aware you are of what words students at various levels know? Try guessing the grade levels of the students who achieved the percentages shown for the following words. Remember that the levels tested were 4, 6, 8, 10, 12, 13, and 16. The answers are shown at the bottom of the next page.

Word	Meaning	Score	Grade
skim	read fast	82%	
snipe	a kind of bird	71%	
spare	to show mercy	78%	
skiing	a snow sport	69%	
skiff	a light rowboat	70%	

What? You got them all correct? You're terrific! An expert! (And pretty lucky too.) Four correct? Almost an expert. Fewer than that? Pretty normal, like the rest of us.

There is another source of information about words students know — the students themselves. What you need to do is build multiple-choice or matching tests for words you think might present problems in upcoming selections. Unfortunately it's a rather time-consuming task, and probably impossible to do for all selections. The comforting thought is that a few such experiences will sharpen your general perceptions of which words are and are not likely to cause students problems.

In addition to using traditional tests, you can simply ask students to tell you which words they already know. Recent research suggests that some students can be quite accurate in checking known words from word lists. It's a far quicker and simpler procedure than constructing, administering, and scoring tests. There are always some who seem to have little knowledge of what words they know. For them, tests may well be the best tool. In any case, tests and asking students can certainly be part of your program for determining vocabulary strengths and weaknesses.

How to select New Words to be taught

You have identified the words your students know and don't know. So what's next? Since your

Answers: 6, 12, 8, 4, 12.

overall list of unknown words is likely to be very large, the question of which specific words to teach is not fully answered. You need some criteria for making the final choice in each situation. The answers to the following four questions can serve as those criteria. Their order doesn't indicate any order of importance, since one may be more pertinent in one situation, another in another.

1. Is understanding the word important to understanding the selection in which it appears? If the answer is no, then other words should usually take precedence for teaching.

2. Are students likely to be able to assign the word some appropriate meaning using their context or structural analysis skills? If the answer to this question is yes, then they probably should be allowed to do so. Apart from saving valuable instructional time for words that need it more, having students use their word identification skills when they can helps to cement those skills.

3. Can this word be used to further students' context, structural analysis, or dictionary skills? That is, can it be used to help them develop a skill they can later use independently? If the answer is yes, then dealing with it serves two purposes: helping students learn the word, and helping them acquire a very useful generative skill. For example, teaching *regenerate* might be useful in part because some students still need to master the prefix *re-*.

4. How useful is this particular word outside the selection being taught? The answer to this question depends largely on the word's frequency. The more it is likely to pop up in future reading selections, the more useful it will be to know. Also, the more frequent its use, the more likely it is that students will retain it once it's taught. How do you know which words will pop up? I refer you again to a fine source, *The American Heritage Word*

Frequency Book. It lists some 86,000 words found in materials written for school-age children.

A further matter regarding frequency deserves mention here. Many commercial vocabulary programs that include specific sets of words err in teaching obscure words when they should be teaching common, more frequently used ones. The student who doesn't know such words as *thrive, tremble,* and *span* (all among the 10,000 most frequent words) needs to learn to deal with words at this level before spending much time learning far more obscure words like *temerity* and *somatic,* both among the 10,000 least frequent words listed in the *Word Frequency Book.* Such words occur less than once in every million words students read — perhaps once in every 15 books.

A final note concerning the four questions: they are not independent of one another. In fact, the answer to one may suggest that a word should be taught, while the answer to another suggests it shouldn't. The final decision in such cases is, and should be, yours.

In summary, New Words represent a good proportion of the words students need to learn beyond the primary grades. Teachers need to become accomplished at identifying New Words that are likely to be difficult for their students, and at deciding which ones to teach. At the same time, they need to ensure that students have, or develop, the skills they need to learn the meanings of New Words on their own. Finally, they have to give students opportunities and encouragement to practice those skills.

New Concepts:
A wellspring of (potential) wisdom

Beyond the primary grades, a second important vocabulary task for students is the learning of New Concept words. Indeed it's a lifelong task for all human beings. All the more reason for children to learn the nature of the task early.

Ironically, the notion of New Concepts is itself a somewhat illusive concept, for two reasons. First, as noted earlier, the distinction between New Words and New Concepts is sometimes a fine one. Words and the concepts they represent form a continuum, as illustrated below.

New Word for a

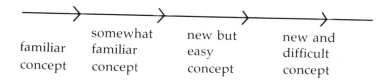

| familiar concept | somewhat familiar concept | new but easy concept | new and difficult concept |

Some words very definitely represent familiar concepts and can be easily explained; others represent somewhat familiar concepts and can be fairly easily explained (at least if they don't have to be explained too fully); and still others represent distinctly new concepts — which may or may not be difficult — and may require a good deal of time and effort to explain (particularly if they need to be explained fully).

The other reason that the notion of New Concept words is illusive is suggested by the parenthetical comments above. That is, the difficulty of teaching a word or concept is influenced by the depth or precision of meaning that needs to be developed. *Fascism,* for example, would represent a New Concept word for most sixth-graders. However, teaching students that fascism is "a type of dictatorship" is certainly radically easier than teaching the full-blown concept of fascism, and teaching students this brief and incomplete meaning of the word would be a relatively easy task. Such an incomplete meaning, however, would be sufficient for many purposes.

A word of caution: as common sense will already have told you, the difficulty of learning words increases from left to right on the above table. New words that represent difficult concepts are very difficult to teach; indeed, one is then engaged in concept-learning tasks rather than word-learning tasks.

How to identify New Concept words

Presenting examples of words falling at various points on the continuum running from New Words to New Concepts is perhaps the best way to show how to identify New Concept words.

The word *lax* is a particularly good example of one solidly on the New Words end of the continuum. It would be unknown to many grade eight students. *The Living Word Vocabulary* indicates that only 69% of grade twelve students knew it. But it represents a readily available concept — careless — and it can easily be defined. The essence of teaching the word *lax,* then, lies in telling students it means "careless." Armed with this meaning, students could interpret "My daughters are very lax about tidying their room" as "My daughters are very careless about tidying their room." And their interpretation would be quite accurate. They would know what I know all too well — that my daughters are absolutely worthless when it comes to cleaning up their room. (In fact, as I'm writing this I'm working up a good head of steam. When I first introduced my system, I used this example of my daughters being lax as an amusing anecdote. Now, three years later, it's no longer amusing. The word *lax* may be easy to teach, but my daughters aren't. If anyone reading this has a solution, write to me in care of the College of Education, University of Minnesota. I grow more desperate each day.)

Further examples of words at the New Words end of the continuum for many eighth-graders are: *scuttlebutt* meaning "rumor," *persnickety* meaning "fussy," and *deluge* meaning "heavy rainfall" or "great flood." Each of these words is readily and quite fully explained by a simple definition.

The word *persevere* represents a different point on the continuum. It, too, would be a New Word for many grade eight students. They don't use it, don't know its meaning when they hear it, and can't read it. Our trusty source tells us the word was also known by 69% of grade twelve students. Yet, *persevere* is further into the continuum than *lax*. It's true that grade eight students probably have an available concept that would be close — something like "continue trying" — and part of teaching *persevere* will be telling students that's what it means. Having learned this meaning, students can interpret "The members of the expedition vowed to persevere until they reached the peak" as "The members of the expedition vowed to continue trying until they reached the peak."

This interpretation would be basically correct, but only basically. It doesn't capture the richness and power of the word. "Continue trying" is rather flat; it doesn't suggest the strength and courage implied by *persevere:* bent back, frostbitten fingers, sunburned face, and aching flesh that pants for rest. Teaching students the full meaning of the word would consist of more than defining it with a short phrase; for at least some students, learning

27

the full meaning of this word would require them to first gain the concept of perseverance.

Some other words likely to be essentially New Words for many eighth-graders, but representing concepts that are subtly different from those the students already have are *demure, obstreperous,* and *opulent.* One dictionary defines *demure* as "sedate," but this leaves the meaning of sedate to be dealt with. *Obstreperous* means "noisy" or "unruly," but people who are obstreperous are also difficult to deal with. *Opulent* means "wealthy." Again, though, the word means more than that. For me, at least, it means extremely wealthy, profusely wealthy, ostentatiously wealthy — the sort of wealthy that most of us will never need to worry about. Most of us are all too seldom invited to homes where we can learn to appreciate the full meaning of *opulent.*

We now move to the next point on the continuum. Consider the word *fulcrum* for grade six students. It would be a New Concept word for most of them. One dictionary defines it as "the support or point of support on which a lever turns in raising or moving something." Unless they have been taught it, this notion will be totally foreign to most sixth-graders. It simply isn't the sort of thing one would spontaneously think about. And the definition by itself isn't going to be much help in getting students to think about it. For one thing, the definition can be understood only if one understands the concept of a lever. More importantly, both *fulcrum* and *lever* are better explained with illustrations and experience than with definitions. Teachers who teach these concepts, and students who have to learn them, need models to manipulate. They need to move fulcrums back and forth, try levers of various lengths and play with weights. Teaching *fulcrum* definitely involves teaching a concept or set of concepts, and teaching of this kind is an involved and time-consuming task.

Predicate is another dilly, another New Concept word for all too many sixth-graders. They might meet the word in a grammar book, and the definition is likely to be part of an explanation of the broader concept of sentence. *English Grammar and Composition* has this explanation (page 24):

> A sentence consists of two parts: the *subject* and the *predicate*. The *subject* of the sentence is that part about which something is being said. The *predicate* is that part which says something about the subject.

If anyone out there has read that to a group of students, or explained it to their own children, and has seen eyes light up with an instant *aha!*, please write to me. You may deserve one of the highest rewards the teaching profession has to offer — perhaps you'll be invited to be the private tutor of Prince William of England.

Your common sense will tell you that to understand *predicate* students need to understand *sentence* and *subject*, and everything those terms entail. Also, they need to understand the notion of "saying something about" the subject. More importantly, they need to understand all of this at a level that enables them to recognize whether or not the "sentences" they write contain predicates at all. So, authors of grammar texts present a variety of exercises meant to reinforce and extend the concept of predicates, and teachers often make additional attempts to teach the concept in lectures and through marking students' papers. And after all that, as we all know too well, some students continue sprinkling their writings with "sentences" lacking predicates, blithely unaware of the concept. Some students never develop the concept at all.

If *predicate* is a toughy, consider *mores*, a word that senior high school students might meet in

ACID RAIN

history or literature texts. Now we're getting far over to the right of the continuum. *Mores* can be taught at various levels, of course. It could be defined as "customs," in which case it would represent an available concept. Such a definition might serve some purposes, although they would be unambitious ones, merely allowing students to get through a piece of material that included the word. In his article "The Concept of Norms," William Sumner, who introduced the term and developed the concept in the late 1900's, called them certain sorts of customs — "customs that are regarded by general agreement as highly important and obligatory as evidenced by strong sentiments against deviation and by severe punishment for violation."

Obviously, mores are not simple customs. Less obviously, the concept of mores is not at all fully explained by the above definition. Fully understanding a concept involves being able to identify specific instances and non-instances of the concept and distinguishing between that concept and other related concepts. Thus, one who understands the concept of mores should be able to answer such questions as "Is armed robbery against the mores of our society?" or "Are folkways the same as mores?" The answer to the first question is "Not really." Armed robbery is against a specific law. Mores are not formally prescribed laws. The answer to the second question is also negative. Folkways are the customary acts of society. Unlike mores, they are not necessarily considered vital to the society or enforced by the threat of severe punishment.

There is a lot more to be said about the concept of mores and the differences between it and a number of related concepts. And that's just the point. Knowing the definition of *mores* given above, even understanding it, doesn't prepare students to answer even the above two questions, let alone provide them with a fully formed concept of mores. Teaching *mores* is not really a matter of teaching a word. It's teaching a concept, a difficult and time-consuming task. And learning a concept never really ends. It doesn't take much of my imagination to envisage a bent-over, retiring sociology professor, all spiffy in his new $200 suit, saying at his emeritus dinner that he had managed to learn only a small part of what there was to know about the mores of his own country. We know that his confession would not be false modesty.

How to select New Concepts to teach

How does one select which New Concept words to teach? There is only one source — the subject matter being taught. Vital New Concepts are those that represent the major concepts of the subject matter. Others may represent less central ideas.

This seems so obvious that no racking of my brains can produce much more to say. The rating of concepts from most important to less important is the task of content teachers. As one moves increasingly towards teaching words that represent new and difficult concepts, the teaching task becomes radically more difficult and time-consuming. It may be possible to take 10-15 minutes to teach ten New Words. However, teaching a single New Concept word may take days, sometimes even months or years, and attempting to teach New Concepts as if they were merely New Words will serve no useful function. It will only confuse students.

New Meanings:
The complex personalities of words

The last category I want to consider is that of New Meaning words. Learning to deal with such words is an important task for both younger and older children, and the task entails more than simply learning the words. It means learning three things: that words have multiple meanings, that the particular meaning a word has is determined by the context in which it occurs, and that the context can help one assign meanings to words.

But, irrepressible academic that I am, first a distinction. There are two different kinds of New Meaning words. First, students encounter words that have more than one common meaning. Second, they encounter words that have one or more common meanings plus another meaning that is specific to a particular subject matter. And, irrepressibly systematic academic that I am, I'll deal with each in turn.

New Meaning words with several common meanings

Run provides a good example of the first sort. It has a large variety of meanings, as the appropriate page in a dictionary will show. One can run a race, run to the store, run a store, and run rapids. The fact is, a great many English words have multiple meanings. *The Living Word Vocabulary* lists multiple meanings for about 10,000 words, roughly a third of all those it contains. Not long ago it was pointed out that between 20% and 40% of all words on basic word lists are New Meanings.

Consider *head.* One can head in a certain direction, put a head on a glass of beer, or use her head. Consider *spot.* It's easy to get a spot on good slacks, difficult to spot a rare bird, expensive to go

DAM !

to a night spot. It's this kind of New Meaning words that elementary students have to deal with most frequently.

However, teaching students all the meanings of all New Meaning words almost certainly isn't the answer. For one thing, there are simply too many word-meaning pairs to teach them all. *The Living Word Vocabulary* lists about 15,000. Moreover, students probably won't need many of the common ones taught at all. It might be difficult to get elementary students to state multiple meanings for *run*, but surely they know what it means to run a race, run to the store, or run rapids. They will learn these meanings and others perfectly well on their own.

What are good sources for New Meaning words? The most obvious is the students' regular reading material. Elementary teachers can scan student selections for multiple-meaning words, especially those that are used with less common meanings, and then explain those less common meanings to students, if necessary structuring exercises and discussions to teach the three things that students need to learn about New Meaning words. However, this is a time-consuming task. Such words don't just pop out of selections, and it isn't always apparent which are the more common and which the less common meanings. You need an easier source, and luckily there is one — *The Living Word Vocabulary.*

Earlier (page 21), four different meanings for *pose* were listed, showing both the more common and the less common meanings. As the list indicates, fourth-grade students are not likely to have trouble with the word *pose* in a sentence such as "My little brother always likes to pose for pictures." However, they may have trouble with it in a sentence like "The heavy rains posed a serious problem." Obviously, *The Living Word Vocabulary* is extremely useful for identifying New Meaning words and for determining the grade levels at which students are likely to know or not know various meanings.

The book is also a valuable and almost inexhaustible source of words to use in exercises and discussions aimed at helping students deal with New Meanings. The purpose of such exercises, however, must *not* be teaching multiple meanings of individual words. Rather, they should teach students that words often do have multiple meanings, and prepare them to deal with such words in context. The most important aim is to give students generative tools they can use repeatedly in dealing with New Meanings. The words in the exercises should be more important for what they demonstrate about the character of New Meaning words than for themselves.

New Meaning words with unique meanings for specific subjects

Now for the second kind of New Meaning words, words that have one or more common meanings and a (usually) less frequent meaning that is unique to a specific subject area.

Product is a useful example. Most school-age children probably know the general meaning of the word *product* without ever having been taught it: something a manufacturer produces. Most upper elementary and secondary students also know the restricted meaning of *product:* the number obtained from multiplying two or more numbers together. They can deal with a sentence such as "What is the product of 4×16?" — assuming, of course, that they know how to multiply. But they didn't learn this meaning on their own; it was directly taught to them. (Note that what I'm considering here is students' learning the word *product*, not their learning to multiply.)

An example of a more difficult New Meaning

34

word of this sort, and one for which the specialized meaning is definitely less frequent than the common one, is *legend*. Most upper elementary school students know that a legend is an old story. While it's true that students learn much more about legends in literature classes in junior and senior high school — for instance, that legends are often believed to be true — they probably learned the common meaning of the word earlier, and without formal instruction.

However, even in secondary grades many students don't know that a legend is also a key to an illustration or a map. They will learn this meaning only if a teacher, probably a history or geography teacher, points it out. Moreover, knowing the more common meaning of *legend* is of little help in figuring out this restricted meaning.

How many New Meaning words of this type are there? Not an overly large number, but enough of them pop up in high schools to warrant teachers' awareness of the potential need to identify those that may hinder understanding. Unlike the first kind, these New Meaning words should probably come exclusively from students' reading materials. Some texts will include key words in glossaries or in lists preceding theme units and selections, and these are likely to include some New Meaning words of this kind.

To summarize, there are two kinds of New Meaning words, those that have multiple common meanings, and those that have one or more common meanings plus a specialized one, unique to a particular subject area. It is particularly important that younger students learn to deal with the first kind, and *The Living Word Vocabulary* is a convenient source for identifying them. The second type is more important for older students; these can best be selected from subject texts.

Words:

So what do I do on Monday morning?

I have used a lot of words to say a lot about words. My common sense has located thousands and thousands and thousands of them. My academic acumen has insisted on a system of classification.

First I divided the mass of words out there into Sight Words, New Words, New Concepts, and New Meanings. I noted the relative difficulty of teaching each of these, and I suggested rough age groups and contexts in which instruction would be most effective. But I haven't said much about methods of teaching the various types. Explaining teaching methods isn't the purpose of this book. At the same time, after persuading you what to teach and why, I should provide some brief directions for instruction.

Let me make this crucial point first. The relationship between a word and the concept it represents on the one hand and the learner's knowledge of that word and concept on the other hand determines which teaching strategies are appropriate. Therefore, teaching strategies, even with the same word, vary markedly, both in content and in time required of teachers and students. Now add the fact that the appropriate strategies will also vary for the more and less difficult words of each type, and what have you got? The realization that, before teachers begin to teach, they must sit down to choose with care. To illustrate the point, I'll describe one or two procedures appropriate for teaching different types of words.

Sight Words

The basic task is to associate what is unknown

WONDERFUL

(the written word) with what is known (the spoken word). To establish this association, students have to see the word at the same time as it is pronounced. If this central notion is kept in mind, then it isn't difficult to think of a variety of ways in which the association can be established, rehearsed, and strengthened. Here are some options:

1. Students must first see the word. They can see it on paper, on a chalkboard, on a screen, on a computer, on a flashcard, in their soup, or (if you can afford it and the wind isn't blowing too hard) written in the air by a skywriter.

2. Students must also hear the word. You can say it, another student can say it, a tape can say it, a computer can say it — or the pilot can yell it through a megaphone.

3. Students need to rehearse the association in order to commit the written version to memory. Again, there are some options:

- Show students the word and have them pronounce it umpteen times.

- Have them trace the word.

- Have them write the word, perhaps using it in a sentence.

- Have them play some games that require them to recognize printed versions of the word.

- Finally (and this is the *biggy!*) have them read easy material containing numerous repetitions of the word. All the other activities will be ineffective, basically, unless you include this one. Readers learn how to read by reading, whatever other help teachers and parents are able to give.

You should note that none of this takes much time for either teacher or student. Learning Sight Words is simply the pairing of the spoken word with the written word. Moreover, the task is greatly simplified by any knowledge of letter-sound correspondences the learner has, and most students have internalized at least some knowledge of them. Note further that teaching a meaning or concept is simply not involved here. Thus, activities that focus on meaning — activities such as having students talk about the word, define it, or draw a picture of it — are irrelevant.

New Words

This is a very different situation indeed, since meaning is at the center of the learning task. Here I'll suggest two procedures, the first for associating a label with an already fully developed meaning, the second for refining or extending meaning.

The procedure for teaching labels is called the Keyword method. Richard Atkinson worked on it, as did Joel Levin and Michael Pressley, and it has been extensively researched and validated. The word *carlin*, meaning "old witch," is an example used by Levin and Pressley. It's an unknown word for most of us, and yet it represents a distinctly familiar concept. It is also an appropriate example, since I learned it using the Keyword method as I was reading the paper describing it. Here are the steps:

- Students learn a keyword. A keyword is a familiar imageable word that resembles some salient part of the word to be learned. The word *car* serves as a good keyword for *carlin*. Students can generate the keyword themselves, or the teacher can provide one for them.

- Students form a visual image of a short episode in which the meaning of the keyword and the meaning of the new word are interacting. For example, students might think of on old witch driving a car in order to create an image in which the meanings of *car* and *carlin* are interacting. Again, students can generate the image themselves or the teacher can suggest one for them.

Now, when students are asked the meaning of *carlin*, the word will remind them of the word *car*, and that word will remind them in turn of the image of an old witch driving one — hence the meaning of *carlin* is "old witch."

The Keyword method requires more time from either the teacher or the learner (depending on who generates the keywords and images) than teaching/learning Sight Words does, because the relationship between a word and its meaning is arbitrary and not mediated by anything like a knowledge of letter-sound correspondences. But it doesn't require a large amount of time, and it does work.

I want to stress a key fact: this method is appropriate only for the specific purpose of establishing a powerful association between an already known meaning and a new label for that meaning. It is not suited for developing, refining, or enriching the meaning of a New Word.

For that I suggest another procedure, one called the Context-Relationship procedure. It was developed by Suzanne Bender and me (1980), and I'm happy to say that it has worked successfully. The name is appropriate, because the procedure places the New Word in context and then describes the relationship between it and a known word or phrase. The heart of the procedure is a brief paragraph that uses the New Word three or four times, followed by a multiple-choice item that checks students' understanding of the word. Here is a sample:

The luncheon speaker was successful in *conveying* his main ideas to the audience. They all understood what he said, and most agreed with him. *Conveying* has a more specific meaning than *talking*. *Conveying* indicates that a person is getting his or her own ideas across accurately.

Conveying means
____ A. Putting parts together.
____ B. Communicating a message.
____ C. Hiding important information.

The following are the basic steps used in teaching New Words using the Context-Relationship procedure:

- Explain the purpose of the procedure.

- Pronounce the New Word to be taught.

- Read the paragraph in which the word appears.

- Read the possible definitions and ask students to choose the best one.

- Pause to give students time to check a definition, give them the correct answer, and answer any questions they have.

- Read the New Word and its definition a final time.

That's the complete procedure. Creating the paragraphs takes some time, but once they're done, they can be used over and over again. Using the procedure itself requires only about a minute per word, and results have repeatedly indicated that students remember quite rich meanings for New Words taught in this fashion.

New Concepts

Methods for teaching New Concepts are different again, of course. One specific technique is an adaptation of the Frayer method, named after its principal developer, Dorothy Frayer (described by Peters). No simple, quick stuff here, as I pointed out earlier. But the method does work well, as extensive tests have proved, for teaching a new concept, a new idea. The adaption of the Frayer method involves the following steps (I have used *temerity* as an example):

- Define the New Concept, giving its necessary attributes.

  Temerity is a characteristic of a person. A person demonstrates temerity when he or she exercises reckless boldness, ignoring serious dangers.

- Distinguish between the New Concept and similar, but different, concepts for which it might be mistaken. In doing so, it may be appropriate to identify some accidental attributes that might falsely be considered to be necessary attributes of the New Concept.

  Temerity differs from *foolishness* in that temerity necessarily involves some element of danger. Temerity also differs from foolishness in that a deed that demonstrates temerity will be somewhat admirable. It is usually the case, though not always, that the danger involved is physical.

- Give examples of the concept and explain why they are examples.

  A person who wrestles a bear would be demonstrating temerity, because normally there is some element of danger and the practice is usually admired.

  The cliff divers of Acapulco demonstrate temerity because diving off cliffs is definitely dangerous and the divers are admired for their deeds.

- Give non-examples of the concept and explain why they don't illustrate the concept.

  Someone who fishes for marlin with a fly rod is not demonstrating temerity because there is no danger involved.

  Someone who drives after drinking too much is not demonstrating temerity because there is nothing admirable there.

WHATCH THE PUDDLES MOSES !!

UH-OH

- Present students with examples and non-examples and ask them to identify which are instances of the concept and why.

  Riding a motorcycle on the freeway without a helmet.(non-example)

  Climbing Mount Everest in tennis shoes.(example)

  Eating a whole watermelon.(non-example)

  Jumping from one stunt plane to another in mid-air.(example)

- Have students present their own examples and non-examples of the concept, have them discuss why they are examples or non-examples, and give them feedback on the correctness of their examples and their explanations.

The Frayer technique obviously takes a good deal of time for both teacher and student. It also requires a good deal of thought on the part of both. However, the fruits of the labor are well worth it, for with this method one learns a new concept and gains a new understanding of a part of the world.

I want to emphasize that, even though it is quite involved and time-consuming, the Frayer technique is by no means the richest or lengthiest method that may be necessary to teach New Concepts. I cite as example my own lack of understanding of the word *mass* as it's used in physics. I simply don't understand the notion, even though I once pursued a brief, undistinguished career as an engineering student.

A few final words on words

Mention of the fact that the Frayer method is not the only or the ultimate method of teaching New Concepts brings me back to the main themes of this chapter — that there are a variety of methods for teaching vocabulary (only a few of which have been mentioned here), that these methods differ radically from each other, and that a method which is appropriate for teaching one type of word is frequently inappropriate for teaching other types.

There are a great many sources for these techniques. Methods texts, basal readers, teaching guides, workbooks, teacher educators, and teachers themselves abound in them. And many of these sources provide really excellent suggestions. Frequently, however, they contain virtually no information about when to use the various methods, what types of words they succeed with, and exactly what they teach. The basic aim of this book has been to provide you with the information and the understanding that will enable you to select appropriate words to teach to students and appropriate methods with which to teach them.

I want to end with one more advertisement for teaching vocabulary at all. It lurks between some lines written by Martin Mann, a *Time* magazine editor. A colleague and I recently asked Mr. Mann to revise a passage from a history text employing the principles used in *Time* to make the text more interesting and readable. In describing his revisions, he noted that the stylistic features he used included "action verbs, contrasts, metaphors, colloquial expressions, familiar tone, word play, alliteration, vivid adjectives, participial phrases, appositives, and a few big words." We didn't ask him to concentrate on vocabulary in making his revisions; in fact, we didn't even mention vocabulary. But obviously Mr. Mann sees the words used as being crucial to writing interesting and readable text. Equally obviously, he is himself fascinated by words.

If we could get students similarly interested in words — really get them to attend to such matters as the use of "metaphors … word play … alliteration … and a few big words" — in their reading and listening, as well as in their writing and speaking, we would, I believe, put them firmly on the road to developing not only rich vocabularies, but more sophisticated language skills and perhaps even more sophisticated thinking skills.

WA WA?